MW01595238

VIVIAN TENORIO

MARINE LIFE
DEPLOYMENT JOURNAL

This journal belongs to:

_____

MARINE LIFE
DEPLOYMENT JOURNAL

BY VIVIAN TENORIO

JAV PUBLISHING

VIVIAN TENORIO

ISBN-10: 0615593259
ISBN-13: 978-0615593258

Thank you

VIVIAN TENORIO

DATE   /   / 20

DATE   /   / 20

DATE   /   / 20

DATE   /   / 20

DATE   /   / 20

DATE   /   / 20

DATE   /   / 20

DATE   /   / 20

DATE   /   / 20

DATE   /   / 20

DATE   /   / 20

DATE   /   / 20

DATE   /   / 20

DATE   /   / 20

DATE   /   / 20

DATE   /   / 20

DATE   /   / 20

DATE   /   / 20

DATE   /   / 20

DATE   /   / 20

DATE   /   / 20

DATE   /   / 20

DATE   /   / 20

DATE   /   / 20

DATE   /   / 20

DATE   /   / 20

DATE   /   / 20

DATE   /   / 20

DATE   /   / 20

DATE   /   / 20

DATE   /   / 20

DATE   /   / 20

DATE   /   / 20

DATE   /   / 20

DATE   /   / 20

DATE   /   / 20

DATE   /   / 20

DATE   /   / 20

DATE   /   / 20

DATE   /   / 20

DATE   /   / 20

DATE   /   / 20

DATE   /   / 20

DATE   /   / 20

DATE   /   / 20

DATE   /   / 20

DATE   /   / 20

DATE   /   / 20

DATE   /   / 20

DATE   /   / 20

DATE   /   / 20

DATE   /   / 20

DATE   /   / 20

DATE   /   / 20

DATE   /   / 20

VIVIAN TENORIO

DATE   /   / 20

DATE   /   / 20

DATE   /   / 20

DATE   /   / 20

DATE   /   / 20

DATE   /   / 20

DATE   /   / 20

DATE   /   / 20

DATE   /   / 20

DATE   /   / 20

DATE / / 20

DATE   /   / 20

DATE / / 20

DATE   /   / 20

VIVIAN TENORIO

DATE   /   / 20

DATE   /   / 20

DATE   /   / 20

DATE   /   / 20

DATE   /   / 20

DATE   /   / 20

DATE   /   / 20

DATE   /   / 20

DATE   /   / 20

DATE   /   / 20

DATE   /   / 20

DATE   /   / 20

VIVIAN TENORIO

DATE   /   / 20

DATE   /   / 20

DATE   /   / 20

DATE   /   / 20

DATE   /   / 20

DATE   /   / 20

DATE   /   / 20

DATE   /   / 20

DATE   /   / 20

DATE   /   / 20

DATE   /   / 20

DATE   /   / 20

DATE   /   / 20

DATE   /   / 20

DATE / / 20

DATE   /   / 20

DATE   /   / 20

DATE   /   / 20

DATE   /   / 20

DATE   /   / 20

VIVIAN TENORIO
VIVIAN TENORIO

DATE   /   / 20

DATE   /   / 20

DATE   /   / 20

DATE   /   / 20

DATE   /   / 20

DATE   /   / 20

DATE   /   / 20

DATE   /   / 20

DATE   /   / 20

DATE   /   / 20

DATE   /   / 20

DATE   /   / 20

DATE   /   / 20

DATE   /   / 20

VIVIAN TENORIO

DATE / / 20

DATE   /   / 20

DATE   /   / 20

DATE   /   / 20

DATE   /   / 20

DATE   /   / 20

DATE   /   / 20

DATE   /   / 20

DATE   /   / 20

DATE   /   / 20

DATE   /   / 20

DATE   /   / 20

DATE   /   / 20

DATE   /   / 20

DATE   /   / 20

DATE   /   / 20

DATE   /   / 20

DATE   /   / 20

DATE   /   / 20

DATE   /   / 20

DATE   /   / 20

DATE   /   / 20

DATE   /   / 20

DATE   /   / 20

DATE   /   / 20

DATE   /   / 20

DATE   /   / 20

DATE   /   / 20

DATE   /   / 20

DATE   /   / 20

DATE   /   / 20

DATE   /   / 20

DATE   /   / 20

DATE   /   / 20

DATE   /   / 20

DATE   /   / 20

DATE   /   / 20

DATE   /   / 20

DATE   /   / 20

DATE   /   / 20

DATE   /   / 20

DATE   /   / 20

DATE   /   / 20

DATE   /   / 20

DATE   /   / 20

DATE   /   / 20

DATE   /   / 20

DATE   /   / 20

DATE   /   / 20

DATE   /   / 20

DATE   /   / 20

DATE   /   / 20

DATE   /   / 20

DATE   /   / 20

DATE / / 20

DATE   /   / 20

DATE   /   / 20

DATE   /   / 20

VIVIAN TENORIO

DATE   /   / 20

DATE   /   / 20

DATE   /   / 20

DATE   /   / 20

DATE   /   / 20

DATE   /   / 20

DATE   /   / 20

DATE _____ / _____ / 20 _____

DATE   /   / 20

DATE   /   / 20

DATE / / 20

DATE   /   / 20

DATE   /   / 20

DATE   /   / 20

DATE   /   / 20

DATE   /   / 20

DATE   /   / 20

DATE   /   / 20

DATE   /   / 20

DATE   /   / 20

DATE   /   / 20

DATE   /   / 20

Made in the USA
Coppell, TX
29 September 2020